1 0 0

CLASSIC

COCKTAILS

1 0 0
CLASSIC
COCKTAILS
The Ultimate Guide to Crafting Your Favorite Cocktails

Sean Moore

Skyhorse Publishing

Skyhorse Publishing books may be purchased in bulk at special
discounts for sales promotion, corporate gifts, fund-raising, or
educational purposes. Special editions can also be created to
specifications. For details, contact the Special Sales Department,
Skyhorse Publishing, 307 West 36th Street, 11th Floor, New York,
NY 10018 or info@skyhorsepublishing.com.

Skyhorse® and Skyhorse Publishing® are registered trademarks
of Skyhorse Publishing, Inc.®, a Delaware corporation.

Visit our website at www.skyhorsepublishing.com.

10 9 8 7 6 5 4 3 2 1

Library of Congress Cataloging-in-Publication Data is available
on file.

Print ISBN: 978-1-62914-703-1
Ebook ISBN: 978-1-62914-839-7

Printed in China

CONTENTS

INTRODUCTION

White Wine Glass

Red Wine Glass

Margarita Glass

Martini or Cocktail Glass

Cooler Glass

Pilsner Glass (footed)

Iced Tea Tumbler

Pilsner Glass (standard)

This book is a collection of 100 classic cocktails, some are relatively recent—the Cosmopolitan, for example, dates only to the late 'eighties, whereas several date back to the 19th-century—The Tom Collins, for example, was first memorialized in writing in 1876, by "the father of mixology" Jerry Thomas in his *Bon-Vivant's Companion*.

The important thing to remember about all of the recipes in this book, is that they are basically guidelines—the most important thing is that you enjoy the taste, and you should therefore feel free to adjust the balance of ingredients to suit your personal taste, or even add ingredients if you wish: you want your barman to be a perfectionist, but you don't need to be!

BAR-KEEP BASICS

The most important ingredient in most of the drinks featured here is the base alcohol, and the quality of the drink will improve exponentially with the quality of the drinks you buy—cheap spirits are cheap for good reasons, so use the best ingredients you can reasonably afford.

Seidel

Brandy Glass

Hurricane Glass

Rocks Glass

Cooler Glass (faceted)

Old Fashioned Glass

Highball Glass

Pint Glass

The same logic applies to any fruit juices that are called for: wherever you can you should use freshly squeezed juice, it makes a huge difference using freshly squeezed oranges, for example, rather than juice from a carton.

In many cocktails, ice is one of the most important ingredients—many cocktails are simply shaken with ice and then strained into a glass. Ice does far more than simply chill your drink: it dilutes the alcohol, making the cocktail less potent, and improving the flavor at the same time. Your ice should be fresh, and if you want the best possible results, freeze filtered water for use in your mixological masterpieces.

Finally, don't worry too much about the glasses—don't be intimidated by the suggestion that you need a highball or a martini glass: feel free to improvise. If you get bitten by the cocktail bug, and want to serve "authentic" cocktails in the "correct" glasses, then a collection of the glasses shown above will cover most of your needs.

Cheers!

BRANDY

Between the Sheets

1 oz brandy
$1/2$ oz light rum
$1/2$ oz triple sec
Sweet and sour mix

Pour cognac, rum and
triple sec into an ice-
filled rocks glass. Fill
with sweet and sour
mix, and serve.

Bombay Punch

16 oz sweet sherry

16 oz brandy

3 oz triple sec

3 oz maraschino liqueur

2 750 ml bottles
champagne

1 liter club soda

6 oz simple syrup

Combine ingredients in
punch bowl over a block
or ring of ice and stir.
Garnish with fruits.

Brandy Alexander

1 ¹/₂ oz brandy
1 oz dark creme de cacao
1 oz half-and-half
¹/₄ tsp grated nutmeg

In a shaker half-filled
with ice cubes, combine
the brandy, creme de
cacao, and half-and-half.
Shake well. Strain into
a cocktail glass and
garnish with the nutmeg.

Brandy Crusta

2 oz brandy

1 tsp Orange Curacao liqueur

$^1/_2$ tsp fresh lemon juice

1 dash Angostura bitters

Slice a lemon in half. Rub the rim of a collins glass with the lemon and dip into sugar to coat the edge. Pare the circumference of each lemon half's peel and add to the glass. Shake brandy, lemon juice, orange curacao and bitters in a shaker with crushed ice and strain into the glass.

Hot Brandy Toddy

2 oz brandy
1 cube/tsp sugar
Hot water or black tea
Lemon slice

Put sugar in the bottom of an Irish
coffee glass and fill ²/₃ full with hot
water or tea. Add brandy and stir.
Garnish with lemon slice.

Jack Rose

1 1/2 oz applejack

3/4 oz lemon juice

1 oz simple syrup

2 dashes of grenadine syrup

Orange peel

Cherry

Combine all ingredients but fruit and shake well with ice. Strain into a sour glass and garnish with orange peel and cherry.

Metropolitan

2 oz brandy

$1/2$ oz sweet vermouth

1 dash bitters

1 tsp superfine sugar

In a shaker half-filled with crushed ice, combine all of the ingredients. Shake well and strain into a cocktail glass.

Pisco Sour

2 oz pisco brandy
$^3/_4$ oz lemon juice
1 oz simple syrup
Orange slice

Combine all ingredients but orange slice
and shake well with ice. Strain into a sour
glass and garnish with orange slice.

Porto Flip

$^{1}/_{4}$ oz brandy
1 $^{1}/_{2}$ oz ruby port
$^{3}/_{4}$ oz cream
$^{1}/_{2}$ tsp powdered sugar
1 egg yolk
1 pinch nutmeg

Shake well over ice
cubes in a shaker, and
strain into a cocktail
glass. Sprinkle with
nutmeg, and serve.

Sazerac

2 oz cognac

Splash of Ricard or Herbsaint

$1/2$ oz simple syrup

2 dashes of Peychaud's bitters

2 dashes of Angostura bitters

Lemon peel

Coat the inside of a rocks glass with the Ricard or Herbsaint and discard the remainder. Add the cognac, syrup, and bitters and stir with ice cubes to chill. Strain into a chilled rocks glass and garnish with lemon peel.

Sidecar

1 oz brandy
1 oz Cointreau
¾ oz lemon juice
Orange peel

Combine the brandy, Cointreau, and lemon juice and shake with ice. Strain into an iced old-fashioned glass. Garnish with orange peel.

Stinger

1 1/2 oz brandy
1/2 oz white creme de menthe

Shake ingredients with ice, strain into a cocktail glass, and serve.

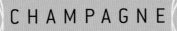

CHAMPAGNE

Agua de Valencia

1 cup orange juice

2 oz gin

2 oz vodka

700 ml cava spanish sparkling wine or 700 ml champagne

Sugar

Lemons or lime wedge

Ice cube

Add orange juice, gin, vodka and cava or champagne to a pitcher. Add the sugar, a pinch at a time. Stir and taste until desired sweetness is reached. Refrigerate until chilled.

Aperol Spritz

4.5 oz Brut prosecco
2.5 oz Aperol
1 oz orange juice
1 lime wheel
1 oz club soda
Ice

Pour the prosecco into a glass filled with ice. Add the Aperol, orange juice and lime wheel, and top with club soda. Garnish with orange.

Bellini

1 medium ripe, peeled and
pureed peach

4–6 oz champagne

Pour peach puree into
glass and slowly add
champagne. Stir gently.
Garnish with a peach slice.

Black Velvet

5 oz chilled stout
5 oz chilled champagne

Pour stout into a
champagne flute. Add
champagne carefully,
so it does not mix with
stout, and serve.

Buck's Fizz

4 oz champagne
2 oz orange juice
1 tsp grenadine syrup

Add to a frosted
champagne flute.

Champagne Cocktail

Champagne
Sugar cube soaked in Angostura bitters
Lemon peel

Place the sugar cube in the bottom of a
champagne flute. Slowly fill with the champagne.
Garnish with lemon peel if desired.

Kir

6 oz dry white wine
1 tbsp creme de cassis
2 – 3 ice cubes
1 twist lemon peel

Combine ingredients
in a champagne flute.
Twist the lemon peel to
release the oil and drop
it into the glass.

Mimosa

1 oz sparkling wine, cava, prosecco or champagne

2 oz orange juice

Triple sec (optional)

Fill half of a champagne flute with chilled sparkling wine or champagne (about an ounce) and top off with chilled orange juice (again about 2 ounces), gently stir. Add a splash or two of triple sec.

GIN

Tom Collins

1¹/₂ oz gin

³/₄ oz lemon juice

1 oz simple syrup

Club soda

Orange slice

Cherry

Combine gin, syrup, and lemon juice and shake with ice. Strain into an ice-filled Collins glass. Fill with club soda, stir, and garnish with cherry and orange slice.

Twentieth Century Cocktail

2 oz gin
1/4 oz white crème de cacao
1/2 oz Lillet Blonde
1/4 oz lemon juice

Shake ingredients with ice and strain into a chilled cocktail glass.

Alabama Slammer

1 oz amaretto
1 oz Tennessee whiskey
1/2 oz sloe gin
Splash of lemon juice

Pour above ingredients into a stainless steel shaker over ice and shake until completely cold. Strain into an old-fashioned glass and serve.

Bramble

1 1/2 oz gin
3/4 oz fresh lime juice
3/4 oz simple syrup
3/4 oz creme de mure

Shake the gin, lime juice and syrup well with ice, and strain into a highball glass filled with crushed ice. Dribble the creme de mure down through the ice, and garnish with a lime slice and blackberries.

Bronx

1 oz dry vermouth
1 oz gin
Juice of ¹/₄ orange
1 slice orange

Shake all ingredients (except orange slice) with ice and strain into a goblet glass. Add orange slice and serve.

Dirty Martini

3 oz gin
$1/4$ oz olive brine
Dash of dry vermouth
2 olives

Stir together gin, olive brine, and vermouth with ice and strain into a chilled cocktail glass. Garnish with two olives.

Extra Dry Martini

3 oz gin

Three drops of dry
vermouth

Olive

Shake gin and vermouth
with ice and strain into
a chilled cocktail glass.
Garnish with olive.

Gibson

1 1/2 oz gin
3/4 oz vermouth
2 cocktail onions

Stir gin and vermouth
over ice cubes in a
mixing glass. Strain
into a cocktail glass.
Add the cocktail onions
and serve.

Gimlet

2 ¹/₂ oz gin
¹/₂ oz preserved lime juice
Lime wedge

Shake the gin and juice with ice and strain into a chilled cocktail glass. Garnish with lime wedge.

Gin and Tonic

2 oz gin
Tonic water
Lime wedge

Pour gin over ice in
a highball glass and
top with tonic water.
Squeeze in lime wedge.

Gin Fizz

2 oz gin
Juice of $1/2$ lemon
1 tsp powdered sugar
Carbonated water

Shake gin, juice of
lemon, and powdered
sugar with ice and strain
into a highball glass over
two ice cubes. Fill with
carbonated water, stir,
garnish with a slice of
lemon and serve.

Gin Sling

2 oz gin

1 oz lemon juice

$1/4$ oz water

$1/2$ oz simple syrup

Lemon peel

Combine the gin, water, lemon juice, and syrup
and shake with ice. Strain into an ice-filled Collins
or highball glass. Garnish with lemon peel.

Greyhound

1 1/2 oz gin

5 oz grapefruit juice

Pour ingredients into an old fashioned glass
over ice cubes. Stir well and serve. (Vodka
may be substituted for gin, if preferred.)

Jasmine

1 1/2 oz gin
1/4 oz Cointreau orange
liqueur
1/4 oz Campari bitters
3/4 oz lemon juice
cracked ice

Stir with cracked ice
and strain into a chilled
cocktail glass. Garnish
with a twist of lemon peel.

Kyoto

3 oz gin

1 oz melon liqueur

$^1/_2$ oz dry vermouth

$^1/_4$ tsp fresh lemon juice

Pour all ingredients into a mixing glass half-filled with ice cubes. Stir well. Strain into a chilled cocktail glass. Garnish with a melon ball, and serve.

Martini

1¹/₂ oz gin
¹/₂ oz dry vermouth

Stir with ice cubes,
and strain into a
chilled cocktail glass.
Garnish with an olive
or a twist of lemon.

Negroni

1 oz gin
1 oz sweet vermouth
1 oz bitters

Stir with ice and strain into a chilled
cocktail glass 3/4 filled with cracked ice.
Add a splash of soda water if desired.
Garnish with a half slice of orange.

Pink Gin

2 oz gin

3 dashes of Angostura
bitters

Lemon peel

Shake gin and bitters
with ice and strain into
a chilled cocktail glass.
Garnish with lemon peel.

Pink Lady

1¹/₂ oz gin
¹/₄ oz grenadine
³/₄ oz simple syrup
1 oz heavy cream

Shake ingredients with
ice and strain into a
chilled cocktail glass.

Ramos Gin Fizz

1¹/₂ oz gin
¹/₂ oz lemon juice
¹/₂ oz lime juice
1¹/₄ oz simple syrup
2 oz milk
1 egg white
2 drops orange-flower water
Club soda

Combine the gin, juices, milk, egg white, orange-flower water, and syrup and shake with ice. Strain into a chilled Collins glass. Fill with club soda and stir.

Salty Dog

1 ½ oz vodka

¼ oz Kahlúa

¾ oz Godiva liqueur

Shake ingredients with ice and strain into a chilled cocktail glass.

The Darb

1 oz gin
3/4 oz apricot brandy
3/4 oz dry vermouth
3/4 oz gin
1 tsp lemon juice

Pour all ingredients
into a cocktail shaker
half-filled with ice cubes.
Shake well. Strain into a
cocktail glass, garnish
with a twist of lemon,
and serve.

The Last Word

³/₄ oz gin

³/₄ oz green Chartreuse

³/₄ oz maraschino liqueur

³/₄ oz fresh lime juice

Shake ingredients with ice and strain into a chilled martini glass.

Vesper

3 oz gin
1 oz vodka
$1/2$ oz lillet

Shake well until ice cold,
strain into a martini
glass. Add a twist of
lemon peel.

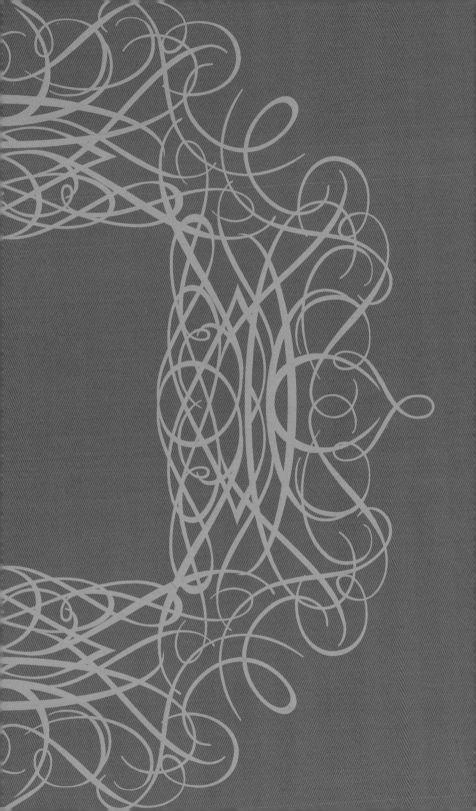

LIQUEURS &
SCHNAPPS

Amaretto Sour

1 1/2 oz Amaretto liqueur

1 oz simple syrup
(dissolve an equal
amount of sugar in water)

3/4 oz fresh lemon juice

1 orange slice

1 maraschino cherry

Pour the Amaretto, simple
syrup, and lemon juice
into a cocktail shaker
with ice. Shake and strain
into a glass filled with ice.
Garnish with an orange
slice and a cherry

Americano

1 oz Campari
1 oz sweet vermouth
Club soda
Lemon twist or orange slice for garnish

Fill an old-fashioned glass with ice cubes. Add the
Campari and vermouth. Top off with club soda.
Garnish with the lemon twist or orange slice.

B-52

¹/₂ oz Kahlúa

¹/₂ oz Bailey's Irish Cream

¹/₂ oz Mandarine Napoléon

Layer the ingredients in a cordial glass in the order listed, from the bottom up.

Blue Bay

1 part Blue Curacao
liqueur

2 parts bitter lemon
soda

ice cubes

Mix in a highball glass.
Stir. Garnish with a slice
of lemon.

Chrysanthemum

2 oz dry vermouth

1 1/2 oz benedictine
herbal liqueur

1/4 tsp Pernod licorice
liqueur

Pour the vermouth
and benedictine into
a mixing glass half-
filled with cracked ice.
Stir well. Strain into a
cocktail glass. Add the
Pernod, garnish with an
orange twist, and serve.

Fuzzy Navel

1 part peach schnapps
1 part orange juice
1 part lemonade

Mix equal parts of each
ingredient in a martini
glass, top with ice,
garnish with an orange
slice and serve.

Golden Cadillac

1 oz herbal liquer

2 oz white creme de cacao

1 oz light cream

Combine all ingredients with $^1/_2$ cup crushed ice in an electric blender. Blend at low speed for ten seconds. Strain into a martini glass and serve.

Golden Dream

2 oz Galliano herbal liqueur

1 oz white creme de cacao

$^1/_2$ oz triple sec

3 oz orange juice

3 oz light cream

ice cubes

Fill shaker glass one third full of ice cubes. Add galliano, cream de cacao, triple sec, orange juice (non pulp), and light cream. Shake vigorously until creamy and strain into a cocktail glass and garnish with slice of orange.

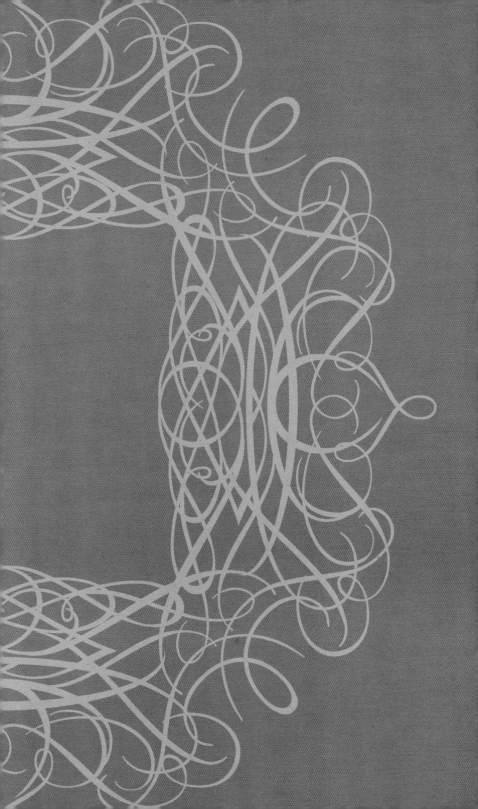

RUM

Bahama Mama

¹/₂ fluid oz rum

¹/₂ fluid oz coconut-
flavored rum

¹/₂ fluid oz grenadine
syrup

1 fluid oz orange juice

1 fluid oz pineapple juice

1 cup crushed ice

Combine regular rum,
flavored rum, grenadine,
orange juice, pineapple
juice and crushed ice
in an electric blender.
Blend until slushy.

Bella Donna

1 oz dark rum
1 oz light rum
1 oz cranberry juice
1 oz orange juice
1 oz pineapple juice

Shake ingredients in a
cocktail shaker with ice.
Strain into a glass full of
ice cubes.

Caipirinha

2 tsp granulated sugar
8 lime wedges
2¹/₂ oz cachaca

Muddle the sugar into
the lime wedges in an
old-fashioned glass. Fill
the glass with ice cubes.
Pour the cachaca into
the glass. Stir well.

Dark and Stormy

2 oz rum
8 oz ginger beer

Pour rum over ice, add
ginger beer, and stir.

Egg Nog

6 eggs, separated
³/₄ cup sugar
1 quart milk
1 pint cream
5 oz bourbon
7 oz spiced rum
Nutmeg

Beat the egg yolks well, adding ¹/₂ cup of the sugar while doing so. Add the milk, cream, and liquor. Then beat the egg whites with the remaining sugar until they peak. Fold the egg whites into the mixture. Sprinkle with fresh nutmeg.

Mojito

1¹/₂ oz light rum

1 oz simple syrup

³/₄ oz lime juice

2 sprigs fresh mint

Club soda

Muddle one mint sprig with the syrup and lime juice in
the bottom of a mixing glass. Add the rum and bitters
and shake with ice. Strain into an ice-filled highball
glass, top with soda, and garnish with mint sprig.

Painkiller

2 oz Mozart White
chocolate liqueur

1 oz Bacardi black rum

1 dash coconut syrup

1 dash orange liqueur

Mix well in a shaker
with three or four ice
cubes. Strain into an old-
fashioned glass, garnish
with a pineapple piece,
and serve.

Piña Colada

1 1/2 oz light rum

1 oz dark rum

2 oz Coco Lopez

1 oz heavy cream

4 oz pineapple juice

Dash of Angostura bitters

1 cup crushed ice

Pineapple wedge

Maraschino cherry

Combine rums, Coco Lopez, cream, pineapple juice, bitters, and ice in a blender and blend for about 15 seconds. Pour into a specialty glass and garnish with the pineapple and cherry.

Rum Swizzle

2 oz rum
Carbonated water
Juice of 1 lime
1 tsp powdered sugar
2 dashes bitters

Dissolve powdered
sugar in a mixture of
carbonated water and
juice of lime in a collins
glass. Fill with ice, stir,
and add bitters and rum.
Fill with carbonated
water, stir, and serve
with a swizzle stick.

Swimming Pool

1 scoop crushed ice
$^1/_4$ oz sweet cream
$^3/_4$ oz cream of coconut
2 oz pineapple juice
$^3/_4$ oz vodka
1$^1/_2$ oz light rum
$^1/_4$ oz Blue Curacao
liqueur

Mix ingredients well,
pour into an exotic
glass and float the blue
curacao on top.

Ti Punch

2 oz Rhum Agricole
Lime(s)
Cane syrup

Mix rhum agricole, a good squeeze of lime,
and cane syrup to taste in an Old-Fashioned
glass. Stir until the syrup is dissolved and add
1 or 2 ice cubes. Garnish with lime wedges.

Tom and Jerry Punch

24 eggs
¹/₂ jigger rum
2 lb powdered sugar
¹/₂ jigger brandy
2 tsp cinnamon
¹/₂ cup boiling water
¹/₂ tsp nutmeg
¹/₂ oz vanilla

To make the base drink: beat egg whites stiff with an electric whisk. Add the sugar gradually, whisking as you go. Add the cinnamon, nutmeg and vanilla. Add in half of the eggs yolks, and blend until smooth.

For each serving half fill a glass with the base mix, add 2 shots of [60 percent rum and 40 percent brandy]. Balance with boiling hot water. Stir well and sprinkle with nutmeg.

TEQUILA

Classic Margarita

1 1/2 oz tequila

1 oz Cointreau

3/4 oz lime juice

Combine all ingredients in a mixer with ice
and shake well. Strain into a chilled margarita
or cocktail glass with a salted rim (to salt the
rim, moisten it with a piece of lime and dip
the outside of the rim in coarse salt).

El Diablo

2 oz tequila
$3/4$ oz creme de cassis
1 lime wedge
Ginger ale

Stir tequila and creme de
cassis over ice in a chilled
collins glass. Fill with
ginger ale, squeeze in the
lime wedge's juice and
drop in the spent shell.

Frozen Margarita

1¹/₂ oz tequila
¹/₂ oz triple sec
1 oz lime juice
Lime slice

Combine ingredients
except lime slice in
a blender with 1 cup
crushed ice and blend
until smooth. Pour into
a cocktail glass and
garnish with lime slice.

Matador

1 oz Jose Cuervo Especial gold tequila

1 oz Red Bull energy drink

$1/3$ oz triple sec

1 oz frozen limeade concentrate

1 pinch salt

Combine all ingredients in a blender with half a cup of crushed ice. Blend until slushy, adding more ice if required. Pour into a cocktail glass, and serve.

Tequila Slammer

1 oz tequila
1 oz lemon-lime soda

Combine the ingredients in a shot glass. The drinker should cover the glass with a napkin and the palm of one hand, slam the glass on the bar or table to agitate the ingredients, and drink immediately.

Tequila Sunrise

1¹/₂ oz white tequila
4 oz lemon juice
Simple syrup
Grenadine syrup

Using the syrup, sweeten the lemon juice
to taste. Then pour tequila and then the
lemon juice over ice in a highball glass.
Top with a float of grenadine.

VODKA

Appletini

1 1/2 oz vodka

1 oz green apple schnapps

1/4 oz lemon juice

Pour the ingredients into a cocktail shaker with ice cubes. Shake well. Strain into a chilled cocktail glass.

Black Russian

1 oz vodka

1 oz Kahlúa

Combine over ice in an old-fashioned
glass. No garnish.

Bloody Mary

1 1/2 oz vodka

2 dashes of Worcestershire sauce

4 dashes of Tabasco sauce

4 oz tomato juice

1/4 oz lemon juice

Pinch of salt and pepper

Lemon slice

Combine vodka, juices, sauces, and salt and pepper in a mixing glass with ice and roll to mix. Strain into a large goblet or pint glass nearly filled with ice. Garnish with lemon slice.

Blue Hawaii

1 oz Blue Curacao liqueur
1 oz vodka
1 oz sweet and sour mix
2 oz pineapple juice

Pour all ingredients into
a shaker and shake
thoroughly. Pour over
crushed ice in a martini or
highball glass, and serve.

Blue Lagoon

1 oz vodka

1 oz Blue Curacao liqueur

Lemonade

1 cherry

Pour vodka and curacao over ice in a highball glass. Fill with lemonade, top with the cherry, and serve.

Blue Shark

³/₄ oz vodka

¹/₂ oz tequila

Blue Curacao liqueur

Combine vodka and rum in a cocktail
shaker with cracked ice. Add several
dashes of Blue Curacao, and shake well.
Strain into a chilled old-fashioned glass,
gardish with an orange slice, and serve.

Caesar Cocktail

1 1/2 oz vodka

clamato juice

3 dashes Tabasco sauce

3 dashes Worcestershire sauce

Line the rim of a glass with salt and pepper. Over ice, add vodka, fill with clamato juice, then add the remaining ingredients. Garnish with a celery stick. Add more tabasco sauce if desired.

Cape Cod

1 1/2 oz vodka
4 oz cranberry juice

Combine in a highball
glass with ice. Garnish
with a wedge of lime,
and serve.

Chi-Chi

1 1/2 oz vodka

4 oz pineapple juice

1 oz cream of coconut

1 slice pineapple

1 cherry

Blend vodka, pineapple juice, and cream of coconut with one cup ice in an electric blender at a high speed. Pour into a goblet or red wine glass, decorate with the slice of pineapple and the cherry, and serve.

Chocolate Martini

2 oz vodka
$^1/_2$ oz creme de cacao

Pour ingredients into
shaker filled with ice,
shake gently, then pour
into a martini glass.

Cosmopolitan

1 1/2 oz citron vodka
1/2 oz Cointreau
1/4 oz lime juice
1 oz cranberry juice
Orange peel

Shake all ingredients
but orange peel with ice
and strain into a chilled
cocktail glass. Garnish
with orange peel.

Harvey Wallbanger

1 1/2 oz vodka
4 oz orange juice
Galliano

Combine vodka and
orange juice over ice in a
highball glass. Top with a
float of Galliano.

Jungle Juice

1 shot Vodka

1 shot Rum

$^1/_2$ shot Cointreau triple sec

1 shot Cranberry juice

1 shot Freshly squeezed orange juice

1 shot Fresh pressed pineapple juice

$^3/_4$ shot Freshly squeezed lime juice

$^1/_4$ shot Sugar syrup (1 water : 2 sugar)

Shake all ingredients with ice and strain into ice-filled glass.

Lemon Drop

1/2 oz vodka
1/2 oz lemon juice
1 sugar cube

Add sugar to the rim of
an old-fashioned glass,
and drop a cube or
packet of sugar into the
bottom of the glass. Pour
vodka and lemon juice
into a stainless steel
shaker over ice, and
shake until completely
cold. Pour into the
prepared old-fashioned
glass, and serve.

Long Island Iced Tea

$^1/_2$ oz vodka

$^1/_2$ oz gin

$^1/_2$ oz rum

$^1/_2$ oz tequila

$^1/_2$ oz triple sec

$^3/_4$ oz lemon juice

$^1/_2$ oz simple syrup

4 oz cola

Lemon wedge

Combine all liquids except cola and shake with ice. Strain into an ice-filled Collins glass, top with cola, and stir. Garnish with lemon wedge.

Madras

1¹/₂ oz vodka
4 oz cranberry juice
1 oz orange juice
1 lime wedge

Pour all ingredients
(except lime wedge)
into a highball glass
over ice. Add the lime
wedge and serve.

Moscow Mule

1 1/2 oz vodka
5 oz ginger beer
Lime wedge

Combine vodka and
ginger beer over ice in a
highball glass. Garnish
with lime wedge.

Orgasm

¹/₂ oz white creme de cacao

¹/₂ oz amaretto almond liqueur

¹/₂ oz triple sec

¹/₂ oz vodka

1 oz light cream

Shake all ingredients with ice, strain into a chilled cocktail glass, and serve.

Screwdriver

1 1/2 oz Vodka
6 oz orange juice

Add vodka in an ice-filled glass
and top with orange juice.

Sea Breeze

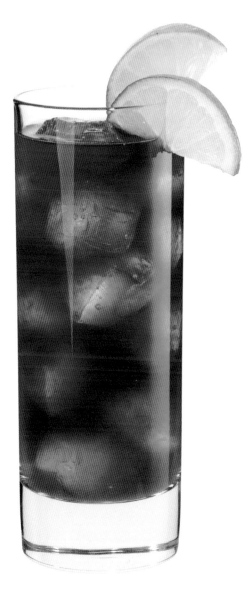

1 1/2 oz vodka

4 oz fresh grapefruit juice

1 1/2 oz cranberry juice

Pour vodka into an iced highball glass. Fill partially with grapefruit juice and top with cranberry juice. Garnish with a lime wedge, and serve.

Sex On The Beach

1 1/2 oz vodka
1/2 oz peach schnapps
1/4 oz Chambord
2 oz cranberry juice
2 oz pineapple juice

Combine all ingredients
and shake with ice.
Strain into a highball
glass over ice.

White Russian

1 oz vodka

1 oz Kahlúa

1 oz heavy cream

Shake ingredients with ice and strain
into an old-fashioned glass.

WHISKEY

BMW

1 shot Bailey's Irish cream

1 shot Malibu coconut rum

1 shot whisky

Pour carefully in the order listed.

Highball

1¹/₂ oz whiskey

Fill with ginger ale

Fill a highball glass most of the way with
4 – 5 ice cubes. Add the whiskey, and fill
the rest up of the way with ginger ale.

Hot Whiskey Toddy

1 oz whiskey of choice
1 tbsp honey
1 cinnamon stick
1 pinch ground nutmeg
¹/₄ lemon
1 cup hot tea

Pour the honey in an Irish coffee glass. Add the whiskey, spices and the squeezed juice of the lemon quarter and top with the tea.

Manhattan

2 oz rye or bourbon whiskey

1 oz sweet vermouth

2 dashes of Angostura bitters

Cherry

Stir the whiskey, vermouth, and bitters with ice in a mixing glass and strain into a chilled cocktail glass. Garnish with cherry.

Milk Punch

3 oz bourbon whiskey
3 oz milk
$^1/_2$ tsp dark rum
1 tbsp sugar syrup
Nutmeg

Shake liquors and milk with cracked ice and sugar syrup and strain into a chilled highball glass. Sprinkle nutmeg on top and serve.

Millionaire

1½ oz Canadian whisky

½ oz triple sec

⅓ oz grenadine syrup

½ oz egg white

1 tsp pastis liqueur

Shake well and strain into
a double-cocktail glass
filled with broken ice.

Old Fashioned

2 oz bourbon

1 tsp superfine sugar

2 dashes of Angostura bitters

2 orange slices

2 maraschino cherries

Club soda (or plain water)

In the bottom of an old-fashioned glass, muddle one
each of the orange slices and cherries with the sugar,
the bitters, and a splash of soda. Remove the muddled
orange and add the bourbon, some ice, and soda.
Garnish with remaining orange slice and cherry.

Robert Burns

2 oz Scotch
³/₄ oz sweet vermouth
Dash of orange bitters
Dash of absinthe

Pour the ingredients
into a cocktail shaker
filled with ice. Stir well.
Strain into a chilled
cocktail glass.

Rusty Nail

1 1/2 oz Scotch whisky
1/2 oz Drambuie Scotch whisky
1 twist lemon peel

Pour the scotch and drambuie into an old-fashioned glass almost filled with ice cubes. Stir well. Garnish with the lemon twist.

Washington Apple

$^1/_3$ oz whiskey

$^1/_3$ oz Sour Apple schnapps

$^1/_3$ oz cranberry juice

Mix all ingredients in shaker with ice. Strain into shot glass, or pour over ice in a rocks glass.

Whiskey Smash

2 pieces lemons

2 – 3 mint leaves

³/₄ oz simple syrup

1¹/₂ oz Maker's Mark
bourbon whiskey

1 oz water

Muddle the lemon, mint,
water and simply syrup
in the bottom of a mixing
glass. Add bourbon,
shake, and strain into
an old-fashioned glass
filled with crushed ice.
Garnish with a sprig of
mint, and serve.

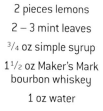

Whiskey Sour

2 oz whiskey of choice
$3/4$ oz lemon juice
1 oz simple syrup
Orange slice

Combine all ingredients
but orange slice and
shake well with ice.
Strain into a sour
glass and garnish with
orange slice.

ACKNOWLEDGMENTS

P6 Shutterstock / Nitr • P7 Shutterstock / Nitr • P10 Shutterstock / maggee • P11 Shutterstock / Serhiy Shullye • P12 Shutterstock / Palmer Kane LLC • P13 Shutterstock / Quayside • P14 Shutterstock / Liv friis-larsen • P15 Shutterstock / svry • P16 Shutterstock / Dmitry Lobanov • P17 Shutterstock / Max Sugar • P18 Shutterstock / svry • P19 Shutterstock / martiapunts • P20 Shutterstock / Greg Nesbit Photography • P21 Shutterstock / Shebeko • P24 Shutterstock / Fernando Sanchez Cortes • P25 Shutterstock / Zerbor • P26 Shutterstock / mama_mia • P27 Shutterstock / objectsforall • P28 Shutterstock / Monkey Business Images • P29 Shutterstock / Novoselev • P30 Shutterstock / Dan Peretz • P31 Shutterstock / Portlandia • P34 Shutterstock / Wollertz • P35 Shutterstock / Palle Christensen • P36 Shutterstock / Letizia Spanò • P37 Shutterstock / KSM Photography • P38 Shutterstock / Dima Fadeev • P39 Shutterstock / Wollertz • P40 Shutterstock / Palle Christensen • P41 Shutterstock / Palmer Kane LLC • P42 Shutterstock / Palmer Kane LLC • P43 Shutterstock / Johan Teodorsson • P44 Shutterstock / Peter Hermes Furian • P45 Shutterstock / Palle Christensen • P46 Shutterstock / Wollertz • P47 Shutterstock / Realmo Muronhi • P48 Shutterstock / Bochkarev Photography • P49 Shutterstock / dondesigns • P50 Shutterstock / Evgeny Karandaev • P51 Shutterstock / Wollertz • P52 Shutterstock / Gianluca D. Muscelli • P53 Shutterstock / Evgeny Karandaev • P54 Shutterstock / Wollertz • P55 Shutterstock / Wollertz • P56 Shutterstock / Dmitry Lobanov • P57 Shutterstock / Wollertz • P60 Palmer Kane LLC • P61 Shutterstock / Christos Siatos • P62 Shutterstock / Wollertz • P63 Shutterstock / Africa Studio • P64 Shutterstock / Soultkd • P65 Shutterstock / Palmer Kane LLC • P66 Shutterstock / Iura_Atom • P67 Shutterstock / Letizia Spanò • P70 Shutterstock / nanka • P71 Shutterstock / Wollertz • P72 Shutterstock / ndphoto • P73 Shutterstock / Max Sugar • P74 Shutterstock / MSPhotographic • P75 Shutterstock / Jag_cz • P76 Shutterstock / Quayside • P77 Shutterstock / verca • P78 Shutterstock / dibrova • P79 Shutterstock / Peter Hermes Furian • P80 Shutterstock / Denis Komarov • P81 Shutterstock / Kasia • P84 Shutterstock / Olaf Speier • P85 Shutterstock / Peter Hermes Furian • P86 Shutterstock / Cameron Whitman • P87 Shutterstock / Dima Fadeev • P88 Shutterstock / Mikhail Starobudov • P89 Shutterstock / Yarkovoy • P92 Shutterstock / bogonet • P93 Shutterstock / White Room • P94 Shutterstock / StudioNewmarket • P95 Shutterstock / Evgeny Karandaev • P96 Shutterstock / HLPhoto • P97 Shutterstock / Bochkarev Photography • P98 Shutterstock / Michael C. Gray • P99 Shutterstock / Wollertz • P100 Shutterstock / Rich Koele • P101 Shutterstock / Wollertz • P102 Shutterstock / 3523studio • P103 Shutterstock / 3523studio • P104 Shutterstock / vsl • P105 Shutterstock / Palmer Kane LLC • P106 Shutterstock / gresei • P107 Shutterstock / Wollertz • P108 Shutterstock / 3523studio • P109 Shutterstock / pixshots • P110 Shutterstock / Palle Christensen • P111 Shutterstock / KSM Photography • P112 Shutterstock / stockcreations • P113 Shutterstock / gresei • P116 Shutterstock / Scaffer • P117 Shutterstock / Joshua Resnick • P118 Shutterstock / AGfoto • P119 Shutterstock / Andrew Thomas • P120 Shutterstock / Kasia • P121 Shutterstock / Max Sugar • P122 Shutterstock / Wollertz • P123 Shutterstock / Palmer Kane LLC • P124 Shutterstock / 3523studio • P125 Shutterstock / Wollertz • P126 Shutterstock / mnoa357 • P127 Shutterstock / Wollertz